Changing ourselves, changing the world

THE 2018 SWARTHMORE LECTURE

CHRIS ALTON

First published August 2018

Quaker Books, Friends House, 173 Euston Road, London NW1 2BJ
www.quaker.org.uk

ISBN: 978-1-9997269-6-6
eISBN: 978-1-9997269-7-3

Printed by CM Print, Brighton

THE SWARTHMORE LECTURE

The Swarthmore lectureship was established by the Woodbrooke Extension Committee at a meeting held 9 December 1907. The minute of the committee provided for an "annual lecture on some subject relating to the message and work of the Society of Friends".

The name Swarthmore was chosen in memory of the home of Margaret Fell (later Fox), which was always open to the earnest seeker after Truth, and from which Quakers were sent loving words of sympathy as well as substantial material help.

The lecture is funded by Woodbrooke Quaker Study Centre and overseen and supported by the Swarthmore Lecture Committee, which is appointed by the trustees of Woodbrooke. It is a significant part of the education work undertaken at and from Woodbrooke.

The lectureship has a twofold purpose: to interpret to the members of the Society of Friends their message and mission; and to bring before the public the spirit, aims and fundamental principles of Friends. The lecturers alone are responsible for any opinions expressed.

The lectureship provides for the delivery of a lecture, usually at the time of Britain Yearly Meeting of the Society of Friends, and for its dissemination, usually in the form of a book. A lecture related to this publication was given by Chris Alton on Saturday 5 May 2018 at Yearly Meeting of the Religious Society of Friends (Quakers) in Britain, held at Friends House in London.

The Swarthmore Lecture Committee can be contacted at Woodbrooke Quaker Study Centre, 1046 Bristol Road, Selly Oak, Birmingham B29 6LJ.

www.woodbrooke.org.uk/swarthmorelecture

CONTENTS

WITH THANKS TO Kathy Alton
Matthew Alton
Simon Best
Gisela Creed
Rachel Hill
Eleanor Meade
Rachael Swancott

INTRODUCTION

My name is Chris Alton. I'm an artist and lifelong Quaker, although I've never formally entered into membership. I grew up attending Quaker meetings in Croydon, then Barnstaple, as well as a vibrant bouquet of Young Quaker events.

As you can probably guess, writing a lecture for a series that holds such historical weight is not an easy task. Being the Swarthmore Lecturer is scary. I have spent months agonising over my ability and inability to: write a compelling and meaningful lecture; coin pithy quotes that may one day end up in *Advices & queries* or *The Friend*; and deliver something deserving of your time and generosity. I am honoured that you have chosen to read this small book. I thank you.

My Mum, Kathy, was a Swarthmore Lecture aficionado. In her last two decades she attended, read or listened to every single one. She died a little over two years ago, due to secondary breast cancer. I still mourn her death and am near overcome with sorrow to think that she will never have the chance to read this. I can only imagine her response to the news that her son would be giving the 2018 lecture. It would have been delivered at a pitch only dogs can hear. She would always tell me of her attendance with characteristic excitement, embodying a level of glee that only she could muster. I do wonder whether she would have been able to contain said excitement and uphold the silence. She whooped with gusto at my university graduation, so certainly had form for being disruptive.

In the years since my mum's death, I think of her in all I do. Her capacity for generosity and love was immense; to glimpse it was to be blessed. I dedicate this book to my mum, Kathy Alton. I love you. Now and always.

CHAPTER 1
Changing ourselves, changing the world

The theme of this lecture is 'Changing ourselves, changing the world'. The original title was 'Being the Quaker you are in a changing world'. But Quakerism is not static. Quakerism is a religion of experience – a dynamic, practical religion of life. It is formed and re-formed in dialogue with our ever-changing world. Our testimonies remain more-or-less constant, the guiding strands that run through the fabric of our faith. There is, though, always room for development. The addition of sustainability to our previous quartet of testimonies is one recent example.

Our testimonies must continue to find new expressions in our rapidly changing world. We too must change in order to effectively answer that which we face now and shall face in the future.

Octavia Butler's novel *Parable of the Sower* opens with the following:

> "All that you touch
> You Change.
> All that you Change
> Changes you.
> The only lasting truth
> Is Change.
> God
> Is Change."[1]

The text comes from *Earthseed: The Books of the Living*, a fictional religious text crafted by the protagonist of Butler's book, Lauren Olamina. The religion in the novel takes root at a time of great uncertainty and flux, and acts as a beacon for community and kinship.

We too are living through a period of particularly rapid change. The impact of climate change is being felt everywhere, but particularly in the global south. In late February the Arctic experienced a heatwave, pushing temperatures in Siberia to 35°C above historical averages. The gap between rich and poor continues to grow. Through a cunning sleight of hand, the world's richest 1 per cent have increased their share of the globe's total wealth, from 42.5 per cent at the height of the 2008 financial crisis to more than 50 per cent now. Austerity continues to disproportionately impact those with the least, and our public services are steadily being privatised. On social media, the most powerful man on the planet casually threatens to ignite nuclear war. He continues to make vile remarks about women, people of colour and immigrants, emboldening white supremacists. In Britain, political and social divisions grow increasingly stark. I don't even want to mention the colonial nostalgia-fest that is Brexit.

Many of us feel disempowered when faced with these vast challenges. It is hard not to recoil from what seem like apocalyptic signs. But we must imagine our way out. We must put to work all the creativity we have at our disposal. We must light a beacon and we must overcome. I hope that this lecture will be one of many sources of inspiration that will help us imagine our way out of these crises. I can only speak from personal experience, so forgive me if I don't fix everything that blights our fair planet in the following pages. It will have to be a team effort. But perhaps I can share some of my tools.

1 Octavia E. Butler, *Parable of the Sower* (New York: Little, Brown and Company (Warner Books edition), 2000), p. 3.

CHAPTER 2
An artist and a Quaker

I am an artist. It took me a while to be able to say that with confidence, without the tone of my voice suggesting an unanswered question. When I say that I'm an artist, I suspect the question that floats to the forefront of many of your minds is, "Well, what do you paint?" Others may wonder whether I draw or sculpt. I will admit that I had a brief stint as an oil painter during my second year at university, but let's keep that between you and me.

My first oil painting was a woman surrounded by flowers. My second showed four girls walking home in the rain. They were very nice. Good for hanging in living rooms or hallways. Having made these, I was working on my third. I was performing the typical image of the artist in the studio, making works of transcendent beauty and genius. Right? As I daubed and mixed and dipped my brush in the foul-smelling white spirit I used to thin the oils, I had a moment of crisis and realisation. What was the nature of this crisis?

As I look back to this moment, through the pale mists of memory, it's hard to put a finger on the exact cause. I know that I was dissatisfied (I may also have been slightly high on the white spirit fumes. Our studio was very poorly ventilated). And as this sense of dissatisfaction welled up in my chest, I did what I'm sure many of you would have done: I denounced painting, swearing that I would never paint again. In order to add some dramatic flair I handed all my paints and brushes to a grateful, if slightly bemused, friend.

The work that I make doesn't fit neatly into any of the formal categories of painting, drawing or sculpture. I am what you might call a conceptual artist.

Conceptual art often gets a bad rap. But to call myself a conceptual artist simply means that I am an artist who deals primarily with ideas. In recent years my work has addressed a wide array of topics: racism, fascism, utopian idealism, British identity, British colonialism, tax avoidance, public spaces, education, climate change, and more. I've made music videos, documentary films, photographs, music, posters, t-shirts, jackets, stickers, banners, cakes, books, a neoclassical treehouse, games and events, and even started a small protest movement. In some ways I'm over my denouncement of painting. In other ways I'm not.

Having cut myself loose from inherited hang-ups regarding what is or is not valid as art, I was able to begin working in a far broader way. I use many of the media that I mentioned previously because of their capacity for existing as 'multiples': endless copies that can be passed from person to person, hand to hand. What use is an idea if you can't share it? The things that I make are made to be shared, and to facilitate sharing. They are – in some ways – the antithesis of the totemic paintings and sculptures that the art market endows with value by virtue of their size, materials, exclusivity and efficacy as wealth reservoirs (particularly when stored in tax-exempt free ports).

More often than not, the work that I make can be carried on public transport. While this is necessitated by the fact that I can't drive and don't generally have the budget to hire a van, it is also due to a decision I made as I came to the end of my first year of study. I produced endless objects that year but discovered that I had nowhere to put them other than – to my shame – the university's skip. Having added my accumulated mass of art objects and other junk to what the artist Grayson Perry has described as a "potpourri of broken dreams",[2] I vowed to vastly reduce the amount of physical things that I made. If I were to make anything, it would have to be easily transportable – ideally on public transport – and if it were to be disposed of, it would have to be recyclable or reusable.

Another reoccurring factor in my work is collaboration. I could not do what I do by myself. For starters, it would be horrifically lonely. Perhaps that's one of the reasons I never got on with painting. It was too distant from the social interactions that we, as human beings, crave. Other people are key to the realisation of my projects. Without them the works would be incomplete. They would remain as ideas in my head or scrawled on a page, rather than as bodies moving through time and space effecting change in the world. I am truly grateful to those who support and enable the work that I do. In recent years I've been fortunate enough to work with anti-fascist protesters, DJs, dancers, sheet metal workers, musicians, young people with learning difficulties, geologists, and members of my own family. For a forthcoming project, I'm hoping to bring together a group of Quakers to form a punk band.

My work asks questions of the world we live in, frequently acting to effect change. It does not shy away from the social, political, economic or environmental conditions that shape our lives and the lives of others. It actively speaks of and interrogates them.

When I look back and take stock of the projects I've undertaken over the past five to six years, it's impossible not to think that my approach to making

art has something, if not everything, to do with being a Quaker. I approach art making as an act of witness, attempting to make contributions to culture that are deeply connected to my Quaker values.

Growing up, skateboarding was a hugely significant part of my life. I often joke that I can navigate the country via the locations of skateparks. In a similar manner, Young Quaker events have been like grammar and punctuation, ordering my passage through time into sophisticated and meaningful sentences. These sentences are writ large across my very being. In no other sphere of my life have I encountered a community that has gifted me with so many close friendships and dear memories.

Alongside the social aspects of Young Quaker events, they also brought me into contact with an incredible array of people and ideas. I am certain that many Quakers of my generation will remember Helen Steven, who came and spoke to Britain Yearly Meeting's Young People's Programme in the same year she gave the Swarthmore Lecture. I will never forget her lucid account of kayaking out to the Trident submarines, secretly boarding one, planting potatoes, then attempting to escape, also via kayak. It is an incredibly memorable, not to mention surreal, image.

The nonviolent direct action undertaken by Quakers and other activists is frequently coloured by a similarly subversive, playful and humorous lens. There is a special place in my heart for the elderly Quakers who have made a habit of crossing the road in a painfully slow manner, so as to prevent missiles and tanks being delivered to arms fairs. It is only in retrospect that I can understand the significance of experiences

and moments like the ones I describe, with regard to shaping the work that I do now. I am indebted to the innumerable Quakers who have put their faith into action, inspiring myself and others to do the same.

I would like to share a brief account of my first Quaker vigil for peace, which I originally wrote for the 2018 Quaker Calendar. I was attending Summer Gathering in Stirling. My mum, brother and I had opted to join a protest, rather than go swimming. I believe it would have been my first:

"It's summer, but I am incredibly cold. It is Scotland after all. I've been sat here in silence for about half an hour, motionless. I'm probably about 13 years old, half my age now. I've been wearing a baseball cap all week, because I tried to cut my own hair and ended up creating a small bald patch. It embarrasses me horribly. A truck rumbles into view. We remain silent, enacting our testimony to peace with bodies and minds, separate yet unified.

Security checks are carried out, barriers are raised and the truck enters the compound. The cold has now reached my fingers, my toes and the tip of my nose, which doesn't normally 'feel' of anything. Meeting for worship always makes me deeply aware of my body and its connection to the bodies of others. People around me are singing – about bridges, about reaching, and about harmony. I join in, lending my voice. We sing, enacting our testimony to peace with bodies and minds, separate yet unified.

Some memories are difficult to recall, others

permeate your very being. I don't think the memory of my first Quaker vigil for peace, outside Faslane's nuclear base, will ever fade. I'll never forget singing as I poked my fingers through the chainlink fence. We held witness for peace at the side of a back road, as trucks came and went, and men cradled automatic weapons. We remained silent, enacting our testimony to peace with bodies and minds, separate yet unified."

I continue to attend Young Quaker events as a volunteer, attempting to pay forward the gifts that this Quaker community has given me. Each year I look forward to being inspired by the incredible young people that we host. I don't look forward to trying to get them to go to bed.

Now that I have given you a brief overview of the ideas and approaches that inform my work, I'd like to get into what I actually make and make happen.

2 Grayson Perry, 'Democracy Has Bad Taste'. Reith Lectures, BBC Radio 4 (2013): www.bbc.co.uk/programmes/b03969vt. Accessed 1 August 2018.

CHAPTER 3
English Disco Lovers (EDL)

I'll start with a biggie. In 2012, while studying for my BA in Fine Art, I began a project that would go on to significantly shape my life from that point until this, and most likely far beyond. Of course, I couldn't know this at the time and bumbled through a significant part of it. I made endless mistakes and did my best to learn from them. The project's name was *English Disco Lovers (EDL)*. It was a counter-English Defence League group, which looked to reclaim the EDL acronym of the aforementioned Defence League. It aimed to reinvigorate the utopian vision of disco music in opposition to a contemporary incarnation of racism and fascism.

The idea had taken root during a camping trip, which I'd taken the previous summer with a group of close Quaker friends. One friend, Gerrard Fife, purchased a supermarket pop-up tent, which he hoped would stand up to Dorset's coastal weather. Upon opening his purchase he was alarmed to find that it came with a flag of St. George. In true Gerrard fashion, he whipped out a permanent marker and proceeded to deface it with a large and somewhat wonky 'EDL'. I simultaneously laughed at his audacity and expressed my alarm. The flag was then adapted to read 'English Disco Lovers'. I believe a disco ball may also have been added.

Gerrard's pop-up tent soon proved to be of little use in the face of driving wind and rain. So it was that I found myself sharing my own suitably waterproof tent with Gerrard and the defaced flag. As teenagers, we'd attended Young Quaker events together and spent much of our time writing and performing songs. These would often be about those staffing the event. Highlights include 'The Simon Best Song' and its sequel, 'Bring Back the Beard'. I have a sneaking suspicion that those songs may well be why I was invited to deliver the Swarthmore Lecture and produce this book. Not because the titular Simon Best is now the head of learning at Woodbrooke, but because writing and performing with Gerrard, as well as other young Quakers, was the crucible in which I began to nurture my creativity.

But I digress. To cut a story of potentially endless meanders short, Gerrard and I continued to joke about this hypothetical group, the English Disco Lovers. I began attempting to form a visual identity for them, scribbling potential logos, in which I subverted the heraldry so often used by the English Defence League. Beginning with the logo, I swapped out a shield for a disco ball and a cross for a dancer. The Latin motto was replaced with, "Unus mundas, una gens, unus disco". As you might be able to tell, I have never had a single Latin lesson in my life. I relied entirely on Google Translate to string together a Latin iteration of the phrase, "One world, one race, one disco", a quotation adapted from Bob Marley's, "One love, one heart, one destiny". It has since been pointed out to me by the artist and essayist Hito Steyerl that if one were to try to translate the word 'disco' from Latin into English it would potentially yield phrases along the lines of: 'I learn', 'I learn to know' or 'I become acquainted with'. It is a happy linguistic accident that hints at and encourages the making of a turn, much like the literal rotation of a disco ball. It is a turn that broadens one's horizon. A perspective-enhancing gesture. So, I encourage you all to disco; you might like it.

In subverting the visual identity of the English

Defence League, it became apparent to me that they were using heraldry in order to historicise and therefore naturalise their ideology. Posting pictures of crusading knights to their Facebook page was a mode of self-actualisation, which involved plotting a line through history. They naturalised their claim to power by extrapolating in reverse. Throughout my work, I have tried to destabilise or subvert the logic of such behaviours, undermining their shaky foundations through humour and play. In the words of the late cultural theorist Mark Fisher, "Emancipatory politics must always destroy the appearance of a 'natural order', must reveal what is presented as necessary and inevitable to be a mere contingency, just as it must make what was previously deemed to be impossible seem attainable."[3] As I discuss my work further, I hope that my interest in what Fisher describes will become more apparent.

When I returned to university and entered my second year of study, I began to consider the possibility of developing *English Disco Lovers (EDL)* from idea through to actuality. What if this group truly existed, I asked myself? What might that look like? What might happen?

In the early days, *English Disco Lovers (EDL)* was a Facebook page. This was soon followed by a Twitter profile. I shared images, captioned with rhyming slogans, known online as 'memes'. For those of you unfamiliar with the word 'meme', Wikipedia defines it as "an idea, behavior [sic], or style that spreads from person to person within a culture – often with the aim of conveying a particular phenomenon, theme, or meaning represented by the meme."[4]

Here are some examples (rendered as per the image on page 30):

"Fewer xenophobes, more disco strobes!"

"Don't hide your faces any longer, come and join the disco conga!"

"People to hate, people to blame. Under the mirror ball, we're all the same!"

People would share these memes with their friends, spreading the idea of *English Disco Lovers (EDL)* across social media, gradually growing the project's online presence and forming a loose community around the goals of *English Disco Lovers (EDL)*. These were set out in a playful manifesto that I affectionately referred to as the 'Disco Statement'. The group's key objectives were: to become the top result when 'EDL' was searched for on Google; to become the top EDL on Facebook and Twitter, in terms of likes and followers; and to make the 'EDL' acronym more synonymous with 'disco' than 'defence'.

For several months *English Disco Lovers (EDL)* grew steadily. I honed the 'Disco Statement' in dialogue with those who had come to identify as members of the community. These were the people who really made the group what it was, transforming it from artistic provocation to a community of subversive political organisers. It was around this time that the project transcended my sole authorship and control, spilling into the lives of others and taking on a life of its own.

Before I say more, I hope you will forgive me this brief tangent. I promise that it's worth it. There are a number of key ideas that run through *English Disco Lovers (EDL)* that I would like to share with you. I'm a bit of a glutton for research, words, and etymology.

My projects are built atop the webs of association that I draw. During World War II, the Nazis occupied Paris. Jazz was deemed degenerate because of its associations with Black and Jewish people. Jazz clubs went underground as an act of defiance. These clubs had to rely on recordings, as live music was too risky. The clubs became known as 'record libraries', or, in French, 'discothèques'. When conceptualising *English Disco Lovers (EDL)*, I looked to these discothèques. They are the original iteration of disco as a mode of anti-fascist resistance. This thread also runs through the discotheques of 1970s USA, which were havens for marginalised people. The lyrics of the genre emerged from these margins, emphasising love, community and togetherness. Pioneers of disco, such as Nile Rodgers, would frequently include veiled political messages in their songs, too. Unfortunately, disco was also a target – a scapegoat – for racism and homophobia.

On 2 July 1979 a Chicago radio DJ named Steve Dahl organised a rally. It was called 'Disco Demolition Night'. It is a famous instance of anti-disco sentiment, fuelled by underlying (and at times explicit) racism and homophobia. The event was held during the half time period of a baseball match. Dahl invited people to bring along disco records, which he would blow up. At half time he marched onto the playing field in army fatigues and took a lap of honour. Before detonating the crate containing all the records that people had brought, he boomed into the microphone, "This is now officially the world's largest anti-disco rally! … Now listen, we took all the disco records you brought tonight, we got 'em in a giant box, and we're gonna blow 'em up reeeeal gooood."[5] Then, in an action that could be likened to nazi book burning, Dahl ignited the fuse. After the explosion, thousands of people rushed the field, tore apart the batting cage and built a bonfire in the centre. It took the Chicago police kitted out in full riot gear to disperse the crowd.

Writing about 'Disco Demolition Night', the *Rolling Stone* journalist Dave Marsh observed that "white males, eighteen to thirty-four, are the most likely to see disco as the product of homosexuals, blacks and Latins [sic], and therefore they're most likely to respond to appeals to wipe out such threats to their security."[6]

English Disco Lovers (EDL) is tied to these histories. It is also inflected with my own Quaker upbringing and beliefs – particularly my belief in effecting change via nonviolent means. George Fox famously declared that he would not fight with outward weapons, saying "Our weapons are spiritual, and not carnal, yet mighty through God."[7] As Quakers, we fight with weapons of the spirit: love, nonviolence, humour, laughter and, in the case of *English Disco Lovers (EDL)*, dancing in the streets.

Yes, having begun online, *English Disco Lovers (EDL)* took to the streets, joining counter-English Defence League protests up and down the country. Having reached a critical mass online, the project had come to the attention of a journalist called Dorian Lynskey. He wrote an article on *English Disco Lovers (EDL)* that brought the project to the attention of tens, if not hundreds, of thousands of people. People quickly began organising street discos and attending protests in Exeter, Brighton, Bristol, Newcastle, Tower Hamlets, Westminster, and Birmingham, to name a few. I remember with particular clarity attending a

protest in Brighton. Everyone arrived dressed in their finest disco gear. Music played and people danced. It was truly baffling to behold, particularly for the English Defence League. Imagine a troop of people bedecked in colourful, glittery clothing, singing along to Gloria Gaynor's 'I Will Survive'. I very much see *English Disco Lovers (EDL)* as an expression of defiant love.

The group continued to grow, and within a year of its inception it had become the top 'EDL' on Google. It had also accrued tens of thousands of followers across different social media platforms, as well as facilitating numerous offline events and relationships. It had acted as a focal point for people, bringing them together to organise around something that they not only found meaningful and cared about, but had fun doing. It is hard to believe that a project of such scale was simply run from my cramped bedroom in North London, via my laptop. *English Disco Lovers (EDL)* was impactful beyond its means thanks to the people across the country who took ownership of the idea and organised local groups.

As well as bringing people together for protests, we began to organise club nights and other social events. Not only did these open the project up to those who wouldn't necessarily consider attending a protest, they also presented an opportunity for us to fundraise for various charities. One such charity actually grew out of a local *English Disco Lovers (EDL)* group. Founded by the Brighton branch, The Hummingbird Project was formed in response to the refugee crisis. It worked in Calais and Dunkirk, supplying and distributing clothing, food, shelter and medical support, as well as running creative activities for children. Since the

forced dismantling of the so-called 'Jungle', the group has worked tirelessly, campaigning for the rights of refugees to be upheld by the British government.

Looking back, I am surprised I had the gall – the sheer cheek – to do what I did. Throughout the project, particularly during 2013, I received constant threats of violence, towards me and those close to me. At one point I think I was receiving around four to five death threats a week. Fortunately, these vile emails have since ceased. As Quakers, we firmly believe in "that of God in everyone". So how does one reconcile this belief with daily torrents of abuse? It isn't easy.

I try to remember that the people involved with the English Defence League are not inherently evil. They are people, and their beliefs – while heinous – are a product of our society. For several years, up until early 2014, the English Defence League was one of the most visible and violent symptoms of white privilege, institutional racism and post-colonial nationalism. Its Islamophobia and racism is abhorrent, and the threat it poses to Muslims and people of colour cannot be tolerated. Its members are minor players, however, when it comes to maintaining this ideological status quo. The major players occupy positions of great power and influence within politics, culture and the media. This is a grave problem; it is a festering wound and it runs deep.

Quakers must be part of the solution. We must use our privilege and influence to dismantle the systems that perpetuate the conditions that embolden groups like the English Defence League. It is vital that we stand in solidarity with people of colour, Muslims, refugees, and other minorities who are targeted and denigrated not only by groups like the English Defence League, but also our own government. We must also look inwards. We have come of age in a systemically racist world, both as individuals and as an organisation. Many of us have benefitted from these entrenched inequalities, as well as our other social and economic privileges. We would be complacent to think that these factors have not left their mark, affecting our attitudes towards others. It is our duty as Quakers not only to acknowledge our own privilege and power, but to use them to actively address these society-wide issues. It is often said that Quakers speak truth to power. Sometimes we are the power to which truth must be spoken.

3   Mark Fisher, *Capitalist Realism: Is there no alternative?* (Alresford, UK: Zero Books, 2009), p. 17.
4   Wikipedia, 'Meme': https://en.wikipedia.org/wiki/Meme. Accessed 1 August 2018.
5   Dave Hoekstra, 'The Night Disco Died', *Chicago* magazine (5 July 2016): www.chicagomag.com/Chicago-Magazine/July-2016/The-Night-Disco-Died. Accessed 1 August 2018.
6   Dave Marsh, 'The Flip Sides of 1979', *Rolling Stone* magazine (27 December 1979): www.rollingstone.com/music/features/the-flip-sides-of-79-19791227. Accessed 1 August 2018.
7   See www.qhpress.org/quakerpages/qwhp/dec1660.htm. Accessed 1 August 2018.

CHAPTER 4
Precarious lives

When I graduated with my BA, I did as many university graduates do these days. I moved back in with my parents. Well, I actually moved in with my grandparents, but this is simply a variation on a theme. It is incredibly common for young people leaving university to move back in with their parents or another family member. While I was unable to find affordable accommodation, I did find a job that had the passing appearance of being connected to my area of study. So it was that I began working as a member of front-of-house staff for two London-based arts organisations.

Unfortunately, both organisations only offered fixed term, zero-hours contracts to their front-of-house staff. The number of shifts that I was offered fluctuated dramatically from week to week and the possibility of being 'let go' at the end of each contract loomed ever -present. Each contract only ever lasted between three and four months, which emphasised how disposable and replaceable we were considered to be. These contracts gradually erode one's sense of self-worth. They also serve to place colleagues in competition with each other. In order to secure shifts and therefore be able to pay for your rent, bills, food, and other expenses, you must constantly outperform others. This state of constant competition has other adverse effects. For instance, it makes it far harder for employees to engage in effective, collective negotiation with their employer.

The workforce is fragmented by its instability. The agitators simply won't have their contracts renewed if they have the gall to ask for better working conditions, regular hours, sick pay or holiday. To further isolate members of staff, a manager even went as far as preventing couples within the staff team from working in the same building. This unspoken ban was one of many moves geared to making the workforce pliant and yielding.

These conditions are reproduced throughout the contemporary world of work and are becoming the norm. While the implementers of such contracts will harp on about the benefits of flexible work, this state of seemingly endless precarity, instability and competition is to the detriment of the worker's wellbeing. Such conditions undercut the inherent worth of each and every human being, reducing them to endlessly replaceable vessels of labour. Such treatment is a flattening out of the complex and nuanced reality of what it is to be human; it is a defacement of the collective soul. My experience of precarious work was a walk in the park compared to the conditions that some people face. I still found it incredibly detrimental to my mental health.

Precarious work and living situations are con-tributors to a wider mental health crisis. While I am no scholar in this field and can only speak from personal experience, I believe that there are numerous other factors exacerbating these conditions. I think this crisis is – among other things – a crisis of community and collective wellbeing. This is in turn a symptom of the broader capitalist system that shapes our lives, placing great emphasis on individuals and their material wealth. We are increasingly atomised at work, during leisure time, and even – paradoxically – when communicating.

The paradox I evoke is that of social media – a technology that allows instantaneous communication but can also make us feel increasingly lonely and isolated. Studies have found that those who spend the most time on social media are twice as likely to feel socially isolated. It can displace face-to-face interactions, causing people to feel as though they lack fulfilling relationships or meaningful engagements with others. This is, in part, due to the fact that social media presents us with idealised representations of our peers and their lives. Such a distortion can elicit feelings of envy, regarding those we perceive to be happier and more successful than us.

I experienced what I would describe to you as 'social media addiction' for around two years. After my mum's death, I went through a period of fluctuating reliance. I was vulnerable and emotionally raw. Social media allowed me to turn away from my problems and retreat into something easy. It was a way of shutting down any semblance of complex thought and losing myself in the endless scroll feature. It acted as a heavy blanket, which I used to muffle my emotions.

In February of 2018, I chose to sign out of my Facebook and Twitter accounts and deleted the apps from my phone. I have only accessed them a couple of times since. I'm yet to kick Instagram, but feel I have a much better relationship with social media now. I am aware of the problems that I and others face, and have set myself boundaries to protect my mental wellbeing. Prior to the 'big sign-out', I'd been using social media constantly throughout the day, locked into a dopamine dependency. I'd be cooking, watching a film or having a conversation and my attention would drift to my phone. I'd go through my various apps, checking notifications or browsing with no specific objective in mind. It was incredibly detrimental to my concentration, as well as my relationships. These stories are not uncommon.

In recent years people integral to the development of these technologies have spoken explicitly about how they engineered them to be highly addictive. Facebook, Twitter and Instagram are all designed to be addictive. All three are major players in what some have called the 'attention economy', which is to say that whoever can occupy the most attention will make the most money.

As I demonstrated when talking about *English Disco Lovers (EDL)*, social media can be a spectacular tool for bringing people together. Other social and political groups use it to great effect to spread ideas, organise events and coordinate protests. Only a few years ago, many people believed social media would prove to be an incredible force for democratisation – a radical, hierarchy-busting technology that would reshape the world. Unfortunately, this hasn't proven to be the case. Social media has certainly played a role in reshaping the world, but not necessarily in the name of democracy. It was instrumental in the proliferation of so-called 'fake news' in the build-up to the 2016 US election. It can produce an echo chamber, otherwise known as a 'filter bubble' that reinforces beliefs already held by the user, rather than challenging them or promoting a critical outlook. Then there are the 'bot armies', fake accounts used to manipulate public opinion. It's also worth mentioning that these platforms are owned by private organisations, which can, and will, do as they please with all the information that they collect. Social media is rife with flaws.

But please do not think that I am down on social media. It is not an inherently bad thing. It is simply a contemporary mode of communication – a tool to be used. With any tool we should exercise awareness of its pitfalls and capabilities, and use it accordingly. I believe that social media is best used to facilitate the bringing together of people, ideally face to unmediated face. It is a poor replacement for a smile or an embrace, but it is incredibly useful when it comes to bringing about such moments.

I am aware of some hesitance regarding the adoption of social media within our religious society. I believe a wider adoption of social media by Quakers is truly vital, particularly if we are to reach out to more young people and people who are not already aware of our existence. Social media is the primary mode of communication for people of my generation and the generations that follow. It would be foolish to exclude ourselves from that conversation.

An ongoing question that we Friends face is: how do we foster a community that is more attractive to, and inclusive of, young people? Steps are being taken to implement this urgent and necessary change. The fact that I'm standing here today is a good indicator of shifting attitudes and approaches. Again, I can only speak from personal experience on topics such as this, but my experience of being a young Quaker most likely overlaps with that of many others.

For a long time, the nature of my job meant that I could not attend Quaker meeting. A higher number of staff were required at weekends, meaning that Saturdays and Sundays were near-guaranteed days of work. Like many other young people, my financial situation was so precarious that I could not afford to say 'no' to working on Sundays. In other words, I could not afford to attend regular Quaker meeting for worship; I could not afford to have the communal, spiritual life that I desired.

Any changes undertaken by Quakers, with regard to attracting young people to the community, must come with an awareness that young people are increasingly time-poor. We are stretched between multiple jobs that barely cover our sky-high rents. Many of us will never have the stability of owning our own homes. We will be perpetual renters, unable to put aside savings, let alone contribute towards a pension.

Over the past six to seven years, I have lived at over 11 different addresses. This made it very difficult for me to form connections with a local meeting, as I would only ever be in one place for up to nine months. This is part of the reason that I've never entered into membership. My financial situation is similarly precarious. I have only been able to undertake the huge amount of work necessitated by the Swarthmore Lecture because of a commission I received last year. I am also fortunate to live in a flat where the rent is relatively low and I can split this expense with my partner. I'm not sure if Friends are aware of how much I have been paid to prepare and deliver this lecture, but the honorarium totals a mere £650, plus travel expenses. If I were to convert that to an hourly rate ... well, I'd prefer not to think about it. I can assure you it would fall well below the minimum wage.

While it is an honour to be asked to give this lecture, it leads me to wonder how long Quakerism can survive on the free labour of its membership. Honour does not pay one's rent. Allow me to be clear. I am in no way advocating for the day-to-day running of Quaker meetings to be taken over by employees. But we do need to develop more robust systems to alleviate the financial strains experienced by young people within our community, as well as those beyond. The social conditions of this country are becoming such that no matter how much my generation values this religious society, we will not have the time needed to care for it.

I encourage Friends to consider the longevity of our faith within the current socio-economic climate, and take measures to safeguard the future of Quakerism. There is already a wide array of Quaker work being undertaken around precarious work and housing. While we should recognise the value of this work, however, there is always more that can be done. Our engagement with this issue can be conducted at various scales. For example, Friends with spare rooms could house young people for free. I know my brother would have found it near impossible to complete his studies without the room offered to him by a Cambridge Friend during the summer. Quakers who are young or do not own property should be prioritised for wardenships at Quaker meeting houses, rather than those who already own their own homes. I am glad to see that this is already being done in a number of places across the country. Where Quaker meeting houses offer rented accommodation, the rent should be considerably lower than local averages. Otherwise we are simply reproducing the same system of wealth extraction that pulverises renters; just because everyone else is charging extortionate rates doesn't mean it's the right thing to do. Ideally, Quaker meeting houses that offer rented accommodation should set rates as low as possible.

The following are of greater scale and ambition: groups of Friends with dormant or disposable wealth could contribute the money required to set up more housing cooperatives for young people. There is also an abundance of skills and expertise within our Society. This would be of great value when executing such projects. Another idea would be to create a hardship fund, accessible to those who need it the most: people unable to find work; people undertaking vital, yet unpaid, activist work; and people with physical or mental health difficulties that prevent them from working full- or part-time. This hardship fund does not need to be solely financial. There are numerous other modes of support that Friends can offer.

Our government continues to shirk responsibility and shrink the welfare state. I am not asking Friends to simply plug the growing gaps. Our approach must be multifaceted. Enable those who need enabling with affordable housing and other necessary forms of support. Simultaneously, lobby the government – with the help of those we've enabled – en masse, loudly and visibly. Use the wealth and influence within our Society to enact systemic, lasting change, within the Quaker community and the world beyond. Set your apathy on fire.

I'm not saying that my suggestions should be hard and fast rules for our community to live by; I'm just asking to live in a world that doesn't profit perpetually from young people.

CHAPTER 5

a shared interest in the bounce

Having grown up skateboarding, I have an accentuated appreciation for the more mundane and functional aspects of civic architecture. Throughout our teenage years, my brother and I would scout out, and become disproportionately excited by, sets of stairs, sloping banks and other instances of skateable terrain. I cannot begin to describe to you the joy that we experienced, thanks to angular bits of concrete. A bench would no longer be for sitting or, at a stretch, lying down. It would become the site of an infinite number of dynamic, creative interactions.

On a daily basis we would rearticulate and rewrite the accepted behaviours prescribed by our built environment, our minds whirring, churning out new ways to interact with the concrete slabs that became our playground. We drew these lines of thought with our bodies. Skateboarding and Quakerism are the twin pillars that support the roof that is my art practice – the roof of my (polite) disobedience and my determination to imagine and remake our world otherwise, in small and grand ways. It is my love of skateboarding that brings me to my next point and my next project.

In recent years there have been various viral scandals regarding the rise of what has been termed 'aggressive architecture'. Such architectural interventions include armrests in the centres of benches, spikes in doorways and studs lining the edges of benches or ledges. It is a particularly insidious mode of design, which exists to prevent so-called 'anti-social' behaviour: rough sleeping, graffiti, skateboarding, or just spending too much time in the public realm without buying something. How dare people consume public space for free, the horror!

Everything must be monetised. A recent example might be the rows of spikes attached to trees in Bristol, in order to prevent birds landing among the branches and subsequently defecating on the cars parked below. Another might be the grid of spikes that a Manchester branch of Selfridges chose to install in an alcove used by rough sleepers.

For me, the epitome of aggressive architecture is a concrete lump known as the Camden bench. Named after the London borough that commissioned it, the Camden bench is truly the superlative in the aggressive architecture genre. Its angular top prevents rough sleeping and skateboarding. It is coated with a graffiti-proof material, and its lack of underside makes it impossible for drugs to be hidden underneath. For the bench's commissioners, it is so imperative that these activities do not take place in locations where the bench is placed, they have commissioned an object that is ultimately a terrible bench. While you can perch on the sloping top, you won't find your stay to be remotely comfortable. The Camden bench is therefore very effective at preventing one of the most dangerous phenomena that public space is victim to, people sitting down. As one's buttocks drift down the polished slope for the umpteenth time, one would be forgiven for surrendering to the bench's will and retreating into the nearest Prêt à Manger so one can get back to propping up late neoliberal capitalism. Well, the planet isn't going to exhaust its resources and become an inhospitable wasteland by itself, is it?

Post-graduation, I'd produced fewer artworks, due to the precarity of my living and financial position.

My focus was, more often than not, elsewhere. By elsewhere, I mean my overdraft and my dizzying £25,000 of student debt. So riled was I by the Camden bench that I decided to make a small project about it, placing this bizarre feat of design at the centre of a new game. Said game – titled *a shared interest in the bounce* – is essentially ping-pong. Players are invited to use the bench's top as a playing surface. Each player has a ping-pong bat and, between them, they attempt to maintain the bounce of a ball against the angular surface of the bench. Instead of competing against each other, they actively engage the bench in competition. It is incredibly difficult (especially when windy) and you look totally ridiculous doing it. But it places the bench in the spotlight. No longer can this concrete slug slump in the shadows. I encourage you to give it a go.

Aggressive architecture deflects what is considered 'anti-social' elsewhere. It does not look to solve, ameliorate or compromise. It is about governing our behaviour in the public realm, often in subtle and unspoken ways that go unnoticed by many. When someone is designed against, however, they are acutely aware of what is happening, and it can breed resentment. In the words of the writer Alex Andreou, "By making the city less accepting of the human frame, we make it less welcoming to all humans. By making our environment more hostile, we become more hostile within it."[8]

I have noticed that Friends House has its own bevy of skatestoppers on the low ledges in the front garden. There are also a number of strangely placed armrests across the centre of the benches, which prevent rough sleeping. Friends, when did we weaponise our garden?

I hope that this question doesn't seem trivial. I strongly believe that such methods of design are symptomatic of a wider society that would rather brush social ills under the carpet, instead of enacting the systemic change that would solve them. As Quakers, we are often part of the vanguard when it comes to campaigning for social justice. We cannot let our standards slip in our own back garden.

8 Alex Andreou, 'Anti-homeless spikes: "Sleeping rough opened my eyes to the city's barbed cruelty"', *The Guardian* (18 February 2015): www.theguardian.com/society/2015/feb/18/defensive-architecture-keeps-poverty-undeen-and-makes-us-more-hostile. Accessed 1 August 2018.

CHAPTER 6
Under the Shade I Flourish

For a long time I was haunted by the idea of forever being 'that guy who did *English Disco Lovers (EDL)*'. While it certainly isn't the worst thing one could be known for, I was afraid that everything I did for the rest of my life would be seen through the lens of that one project. I also feared that I would never do anything as 'good' as *English Disco Lovers (EDL)*, despite how vague or subjective the metric of 'good' is. I recall my friend Sam Walton describing this fear to me as 'second album syndrome', that difficulty of overcoming the expectations created by your first album – or in my case, project.

I began to put some space between myself and *English Disco Lovers (EDL)*. I could no longer be the caretaker of a project that – in my opinion – had run its creative course and descended into a protracted administrative task. There are various people who continue to run events under the banner, but, for me, it was time to let go and move on. With distance came the ability to be self-critical. Through the act of looking back, observing the project from the outside, rather than being entrenched within it, I could see the flaws and gaps – the unresolved ideas to which one could return and explore further. The adage of satirists everywhere, 'always punch up' rang clear as a bell.

While the seed of this thought had long nestled in my mind, it was only with distance that it could bloom. To 'punch up' is to target the dominant group – those with higher levels of power in terms of status, capital or privilege. When it comes to dismantling white privilege, institutional racism and post-colonial nationalism, the most effective punches are levelled at their foundations. Or, as my mum would always remind my brother and I when we weeded the garden, to stop weeds spreading you must tackle the roots. It was with this mindset that I embarked upon my next project.

Under the Shade I Flourish began with a chance encounter with a double life-size bust of Michael Ashcroft. "Where might I find such a bust?", I hear you cry. I know you would all love one for your living room or garden or perhaps both. Well, said bust was in the foyer of Anglia Ruskin University, where my brother Matt was studying at the time. As I'm sure many of you are aware, Michael Ashcroft is a former member of the House of Lords and former chair of the Conservative Party. His estimated net worth is $1.73 billion and he is known to have avoided tax. Thanks to the recent Paradise Papers leak, we now know for a fact that he was domiciled in Belize for tax purposes while he was a member of the House of Lords.

Fewer of you will be familiar with Michael Ashcroft's escapades during the 1960s. As well as selling tickets for boxing matches on the black market, he managed a rhythm 'n' blues band called Trident. Quakers in particular will associate the word 'trident' with the UK's nuclear weapons programme. It's interesting how that word has moved through time. Tridents have been wielded by the likes of Poseidon, Neptune and Britannia. The latter inherited hers from Neptune, as a form of divine justification for Britain expanding its empire. Today the trident maintains an affiliation with neo-colonial practices such as tax avoidance. The Trident Trust, a fiduciary catering for companies and rich individuals, operates out of various locations including Panama, the Virgin Islands, Guernsey, and Luxembourg.

Returning to Trident, the rhythm 'n' blues band, I discovered this snippet of information in a first edition copy of Ashcroft's autobiography. Said snippet appears in no other edition of the book, so he either deemed it irrelevant or information worthy of hiding. He managed the band for no more than a few months, driving them from gig to less-than-packed gig, all the while hoping that they would one day achieve the same level of commercial success as the Beatles.

I was particularly taken with the idea that Michael Ashcroft may well have remained Trident's manager, had the band achieved his desired degree of success. In an alternative universe things could have turned out differently. Michael Ashcroft would never have entered business or politics. Instead of becoming a cleaning company tycoon and big-time political player, he would have managed a rhythm 'n' blues band. I began to imagine this alternative timeline.

As I tried to write this section, it became apparent to me why I am an artist rather than a writer. I simply do not possess the ability to express complexity and ambiguity with clarity in my writing (or, at least, I've spent very little time honing this ability). There are so many things at play in *Under the Shade I Flourish* that it's not only incredibly difficult, but incredibly boring for me to unpack the project for you and describe its intricacies at length. So, on the opposite page is the project as a diagram, a mind map of associated places, people, objects, historical events, mythology, Latin mottos, and more.

This mind map ties together Britain's colonial history with contemporary tax avoidance, as well as the rhythm 'n' blues genre. The third seems a little incongruous,

but it's worth remembering how the so-called 'British Invasion' was reported. In early 1964 *Life* magazine put it like this: "In [1776] England lost her American colonies. Last week the Beatles took them back."[9] As well as being described in this manner, the music of bands like the Beatles and the Rolling Stones was derived from the work of black musicians who never achieved the same level of critical success, despite pioneering the genre.

I used all of these connections to inform Trident's story and music, weaving a fiction around them and using this fiction as a tool for articulating a wider truth. In the narrative of the project Trident release their first single, which proves to be a hit in British Honduras. The A-side is titled 'Safe Haven', the B-side is 'Under the Shade I Flourish'. Building on its initial success, the group tours throughout Central America and the Caribbean, as well as releasing an album. All of the tracks riff on tax avoidance terminology or the lyrics to national anthems.

The project is about exploring an attitude, a history and a tendency rather than a set of concrete facts. Different near-invisible strains of colonialism run through multiple phenomena. By bringing these into contact with each other, this truth can be seen with greater clarity.

9   Parke Puterbaugh, 'The British Invasion: From the Beatles to the Stones, the Sixties Belonged to Britain', *Rolling Stone* magazine (14 July 1988): www.rollingstone.com/music/news/the-british-invasion-from-the-beatles-to-the-stones-the-sixties-belonged-to-britain-19880714. Accessed 1 August 2018.

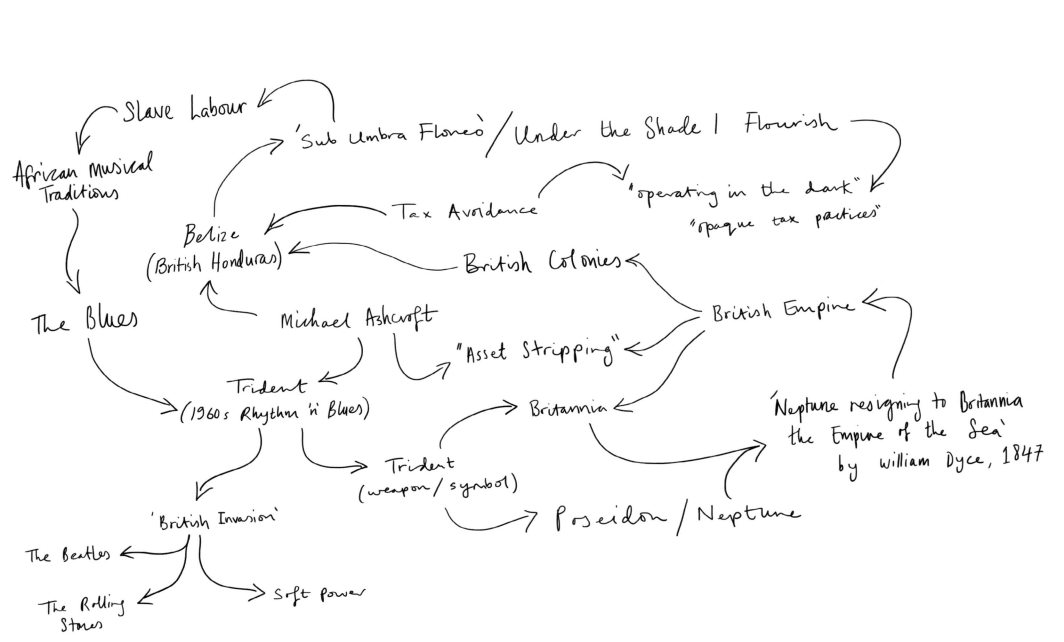

Slave Labour

'Sub Umbra Floreo' / Under the Shade I Flourish

African Musical Traditions

"operating in the dark"
"opaque tax practices"

Tax Avoidance

Belize
(British Honduras)

British Colonies

The Blues

Michael Ashcroft

British Empire

"Asset Stripping"

Trident
(1960s Rhythm 'n' Blues)

Britannia

'Neptune resigning to Britannia
the Empire of the Sea'
by William Dyce, 1847

Trident
(weapon / symbol)

Poseidon / Neptune

'British Invasion'

The Beatles

The Rolling Stones

Soft Power

CHAPTER 7
Crudely Plucking the Strings

Much of what I do is not commissioned, though the occasional invitation does come though. The next project arose from one such invitation, which I received at the beginning of 2018. A small artist-run gallery and skatepark called Spit & Sawdust, which is in Cardiff, asked me to produce an artwork for its external billboard. For an artist at my level, paid opportunities are few and far between. I also quite fancied the idea of doing a billboard. So I gratefully accepted.

I had been thinking about the Bristol Channel for a while. More precisely, I had been thinking about the 1607 flood of the Bristol Channel, which some hypothesise to have been caused by a tsunami. This catastrophic event inundated the landscape that surrounded the channel with tonnes upon tonnes of rushing water. Thousands of humans and animals died. Cardiff was the most badly affected town. In conjunction with this historical flood, I had also been thinking about the new nuclear power station being built on the shore of the Channel, namely Hinkley Point C. I saw this opportunity to think about these ideas simultaneously: climate change, extreme weather and nuclear power.

The science fiction writer J.G. Ballard once remarked that he "always thought that people living in the cosy suburbia of Western Europe and America never appreciated just how vulnerable we were to climate disasters."[10] We are cosy, especially compared to the Global South, which is disproportionately affected by climate change and climate disasters. We have it incredibly easy, and it has made us complacent. I decided to try to create a six metre by three metre warning, an omen of what may come to pass without drastic action.

One of the few surviving visual records of the flood is a simple woodcut depicting people and animals floating in the water. Some scramble up trees to safety, others sit atop houses. A church occupies the centre of the image. In my version, the church has been replaced by Hinkley Point C as it undergoes a flood-induced meltdown. This small gesture of replacing one building with another was meant as a direct comment about where contemporary faith resides. We would be fools to place our faith in nuclear power, particularly that which is generated by Hinkley. Numerous scientists have published reports linking Hinkley to the renewal of the Trident nuclear weapons system. They describe the power station as a means by which electricity consumers will subsidise military nuclear infrastructure

The sheer absurdity of Hinkley is irrefutable. Once complete, it will be the most expensive power station in the world. The production of nuclear power does not contribute to carbon emissions, but research suggests that "British low-carbon energy strategies are more expensive than they need to be".[11] This is due to the aforementioned desire to fund Trident surreptitiously. So Hinkley is even implicated in climate change. The £19.6 billion power station will perch on the edge of a precipice, vulnerable to instances of extreme weather which are becoming more frequent and being further generated by the UK's nuclear programme.

---

10 J.G. Ballard to Travis Elborough. 'Reality is a Stage Set', interview with J.G. Ballard, appendix in *The Drowned World* (London: Harper Perennial, 1962 (7th edition, 2008)).

11 'British attachment to nuclear submarines drives bias towards nuclear power', Science Policy Research Unit (SPRU), University of Sussex website, 21 September 2016: www.sussex.ac.uk/broadcast/read/36984. Accessed 1 August 2018.

CHAPTER 8
A currency backed by atmospheric carbon

I am often the first to admit that the works I make are never perfect. There are always problems. I often develop successive projects, each of which addresses the issues present in those that preceded. All the works speak to each other, particularly to each other's flaws or blind spots. My work for the billboard, like everything I've made and everything I'll ever make, is flawed. But being flawed doesn't necessarily stop me, otherwise I would render myself immobile. You have to try. In trying comes the opportunity to learn, regardless of success or failure. In a beautiful essay called 'The White Bird', John Berger wrote that art "proclaims man in the hope of receiving a surer reply."[12] I love the image of Berger bellowing proclamations into the unknown, then straining to hear a response that may never come. I originally read this text in 2013, but that image has stayed with me.

For Berger, making art is about the attempt to better know ourselves and the world. It's about grappling with what it is to live and what it is to live now, without the promise of definitive answers. We are all dealing with the uncertain, the unknown and the unknowable. Art is one of the many responses humans have with regard to our uncertain existence; another is attending Quaker meeting, or any other form of religious or ritualised gathering.

In the face of the abyss, we reach out to others who, like ourselves, do not know. We weave a web of love, friendship and kindness – a network of meaning that makes us feel less like we're on a tiny lump of rock, hurtling through space, and more like we're holding hands with those we care for and who care for us. We have faith that there is something beyond our immediate perception – something we occasionally glimpse when we gather.

So why do I describe the image I've produced for the billboard as flawed? Because it presents an image of the apocalypse. While I could try to dodge this problem by describing it as a warning or an omen, our literary and visual culture is already full of this kind of imagery. It is frightening to think about how much of our visual culture regarding climate change is fixated upon the apocalyptic. How many films can you think of that are about people successfully averting climate change? None. That plot line wouldn't exactly make for a box office hit. They're all about massive unstoppable waves, snowstorms or droughts. Others are about fleeing to Mars. Such images are not conducive to action. They cause people to shrink back from the sheer enormity of the task in hand by making climate change seem like a foregone conclusion. Presenting the annihilation of our species as inevitable does nothing to halt our charge towards it. Proposing that we all fly away to Mars only abdicates responsibility for the climate horrors we continue to inflict upon this planet.

How do I intend to address this flaw? The answer is obvious. I must develop a currency that will continually depreciate in value. A joke. But I'm also serious.

I'm sure many of you have heard about Bitcoin. It is described as a decentralised cryptocurrency. Transactions are recorded publicly, and cryptography secures these transactions. There is a lot that could be said about Bitcoin, but I won't bore you with all the details. Personally, I'm interested in how much energy is required to produce bitcoins. Bitcoins are produced as a reward for a process called 'mining'. In Bitcoin mining facilities, stacks of hundreds if not thousands of computers run around the clock. Enormous fans pull cold air through the buildings to cool the machines, which expel huge amounts of heat as they run endless calculations. The mining of bitcoins consumes a colossal amount of electricity. It's been reported to be as high as 42 terawatt hours per annum, which equates to approximately 20 megatonnes of CO_2, or one million transatlantic flights. If bitcoin miners were a country, they would be the 48th highest consumers of energy in the world. Without getting into a lot of technical terminology, the accelerated consumption of energy is embedded within the core of Bitcoin.

The economist and Quaker Kenneth E. Boulding once said that, "Anyone who believes in indefinite growth of anything physical on a physically finite planet is either a madman or an economist."[13] Global economies are predicated on perpetual growth. Left unchecked, our fixation with resource consumption will devastate our planet. The wellbeing of a country is measured by its Gross Domestic Product (GDP). If this number ceases to increase or, horror of horrors, begins to decrease, it is considered a disaster. So infatuated are we with growth that a decrease in GDP is described as negative growth. Soon after his re-election, and in the wake of Hurricane Sandy, Barack Obama even remarked that "[W]e're [not] going to ignore jobs and growth simply to address climate change."[14] It seems utterly bizarre that growth and the creation of jobs should be prioritised over the annihilation of our planet. So I figured that developing a currency that implicates such economic practices in the ongoing process of climate change might be a good idea.

Until 1931 the UK used a gold standard, a monetary system where the value of a currency is linked to gold. What if the value of a currency was directly linked to an indicator of climate change? Such indicators include: arctic sea ice, sea levels, and atmospheric carbon. By now, you're probably aware that I'm not an economist. I plan to seek out expert advice in order to establish a working model for this currency, but my train of thought thus far is as follows: I intend to create a currency that is directly linked to an indicator of climate change. This would produce a feedback loop, linking the currency's value to the indicator. If the currency's value was directly linked to the amount of atmospheric carbon, this feedback loop would cause the currency to depreciate in value if the amount of atmospheric carbon increased. This model may well be far too simplistic. It is perhaps necessary to derive some kind of metric from these indicators of climate change, to which the currency could then be linked.

Either way, I hope to create a currency that discourages investment in that which would exacerbate climate change (for example, fracking and offshore drilling) and encourages investment in that which would slow or halt climate change (like solar energy and wind farms). Unfortunately for anyone choosing to purchase this currency, it is likely to continually depreciate in value – unless we get our act together.

12 John Berger, 'The White Bird', in *Why Look at Animals?* (London: Penguin Books, 2009).
13 Quoted in: Dave Pruett, 'The Myth of Exponential Growth', *The Huffington Post* (3 October 2013): www.huffingtonpost.com/dave-pruett/the-myth-of-exponential-growth_b_4037025.html. Accessed 1 August 2018.
14 Ibid.

CHAPTER 9
Imagining the world otherwise

You may well think the projects that I have described to you are absurd. But I think we should spend more time investigating such absurdities. While a currency that constantly depreciates in value may seem ridiculous, a currency that plays a part in curtailing climate change would be miraculous. The absurd is defined by the dominant logic of our time, and that dominant logic has led us to a dead end. It insists, though, that we forge ahead. To be absurd is to go against or think outside of this flawed, dead-end logic, which tries to present itself as the natural way, the way things must be, or the only way – the way things will forever be.

In many ways, being an artist grants me licence to pursue that which might otherwise be deemed pointless or impossible. When I founded *English Disco Lovers* (*EDL*) my tutors were not only puzzled, but actively sought to discourage my pursuit of the project. But the pursuit of ideas that sit outside of the norm (or even go against it) are vital. Without them, we are destined to remain static – or worse, go in the wrong direction.

Without new ideas that defy the norm, we are locked into modes of thought that have failed us, and we will fail to create a better world from such poor resources.

I think of my work as a series of exercises in imagining otherwise – the world otherwise, ourselves otherwise – and acting to make that seemingly distant or intangible otherwise more possible, to bring it closer to hand. These are my tools, I offer them to you. May we go forth and reshape the world. May our exploits be worthy of the first blockbuster film to tell the tale of a civilisation that averted climate change, of a people who dismantled entrenched social inequalities of class, race, gender, sexuality, and more; a people who learnt to live in peace with the needs of all, catered for within the limits of our planet. Let it tell a story not of heroes, but of communities that forged our future anew. We must imagine this future, for, if we cannot imagine it, we cannot speak it into existence.

LIST OF ILLUSTRATIONS

Fewer xenophobes! More disco strobes!

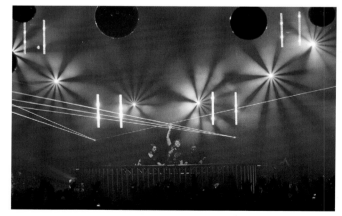